222

222
A Book of Signs

KHALIL ISHMAEL GRIFFITH

The Reel, LLC

Copyright © 2021 by Khalil Ishmael Griffith

All words and images are the intellectual property of the author unless otherwise stated.

All rights reserved. No part of this book may be reproduced in any manner whatsoever without written permission except in the case of brief quotations embodied in critical articles and reviews.

First Printing, 2021

Contents

Copyright	iv
Acknowledgments	vii
Foreword	ix

Nobody knows what they're doing.	2
It's okay to not know everything.	7
Fall in love with yourself.	11
Pain is a natural occurrence.	17
Your words hold weight.	21
What do you value?	27
We're all learning.	34
It is what it is.	40
Did you take a breath today?	49

Dispel your doubt.	56
You will fail.	66
It's okay to change your mind.	73
The world will still be here tomorrow.	81
Live.	86
You'll figure it out along the way.	92
It's okay to put yourself first.	99
You are what you eat.	105
See the good in every situation.	112
Change is the only constant.	120
Your will is your own.	130
About the Author	134
Khalil's Sign	137
An Expression of Gratitude	139

Acknowledgments

Thank *you* for buying this book, of course, but more importantly, thanks for making it this far. You're here because you want to be here. This book is for you. You are acknowledged. For your growth, strength, for being the best you that you can be.

I'd also like to take this brief moment to thank everyone that contributed to the creation of this book. Every friend, family, and stranger. 222 would not be what it is without any of you. Shunydra (for pushing the idea and supporting me every step of the way). Ashston (for pushing me when I didn't want to take a mother step, making all of this possible, and the many, many typos). Celestine (for helping me find even more typos), Khali (for helping me figure everything out and listening to me whine), Brennan (for the support and grounding words), Kamarri (for support and contribution) Kris Keaton (for support and contribution), Liyah (for contribution), Rajah (for thoughts, support, and contribution), Kabriya (for support and contribution), Adrianna (for support and contribution), Kiauna (for support and contribution), Jerryll (for contribution) Sydney (for contribution,, support, and suggestions) my dad (for literally everything), my mom (for always encouraging and supporting me and helping make the events and coverage of the book possible), Courtney (for contributions and support), Katie (for giving me a new perspective when I first started the book), Duryan (for contributions and inspiration), Tsukiyomi (for contributions and a new lens through which I can view life and my work), Isaiah Rashad (for the unexpected contribution and constant inspiration), Stoney (for contributions), Daja (for the constant love and support), Joe (for always checking in and waking me up in the oddest ways), Damian (for support and contribution), Tyren (for the support and contribution), Iris (for constant support and contribution), Jasmine (for support and contribution), J'La (for support and contribution), Jalen (for support, advice and suggestions), Sully (for support and contribution), Ty (for support and contribution), Faerybru (for support and contribution), Kyle (for support and contribution), Stoney, (for support and contribution), Jayla (for support and contribution), Peanut (for support and contribution), Nevay (for support and contribution), Koopa (for support and contribution), and Truman (for support and contribution). Also thank you to everyone that took the time to read the book before its release and letting me know that I was moving in the right direction. Another round of thanks to everyone who has supported me and my many facets of expression over the years. I couldn't imagine making it this far without any of you. Thank you.

Foreword

This book was made for you. Admittedly though, it didn't start off that way.

I was dealing with a lot in my personal life at the time of the conception of this book. I was picking myself up off the floor after what felt like the biggest romantic blunder of my life, handling an identity crisis, and juggling a bunch of other unimportant things all while attempting to claim my place in this world. It was a lot, and at some point in this process, I hit rock bottom. Everything fell apart and I felt like I had no one, so I started writing to myself. Asking myself questions, and writing down what I felt at the time. It felt pointless at first, but I kept writing. I wrote through all the things that ate at my spirit. I wrote through my heartbreak, confusion of self, and all the other minuscule things that felt as if they were bigger than me. Through my pen, I created a stream of consciousness that answered every question and created a solution for everything I was dealing with.

While writing for what felt like hours I realized that every answer to every question I had was simple in nature. Every resolution was something that felt like it had always been there – like things I'd seen or heard before. But in reality, those answers and solutions were there all along, they just didn't mean much to me before. No matter what advice someone gave me in regards to my reality, it didn't matter. Why? Because I wasn't ready to acknowledge what I was given as a truth of *my* reality. In other words, *a sign isn't a sign until you see it as one.*

After this discovery, I also realized no one can make anyone change. No one can make you do – or even see – what the "right" thing may be until you're ready to acknowledge it as such. This epiphany was disheartening. Watching someone suffer at the hands of their own reality is tough, especially when there's an alternative to the cycle of problems they endure. How do you make a horse drink the water after you lead it to it? After being dumbfounded for days, I was finally able to answer the question. It's not really about when a horse drinks water, but the fact that the water is there. When it's thirsty, it will drink. When we are ready for a change, we will change. This is when I knew exactly what I was going to do, I'd write a book. I knew exactly what I wanted it to be: a sign for a friend in a bind, or for a brother that feels lost, or maybe even for a stranger who's looking for something. There was a huge chance that the pages in it would be nothing to them initially, but a week from now? A month? Even a year? It could mean the world to them.

With a countless number of impactful people in my life, I knew I couldn't just leave something like this to myself. I couldn't possibly find and share every sign, because I was and (and I'm still) learning. After creating the husk of the book I asked those I loved, adored, or met in passing: "What sign do you want to leave for others? And that's how 222 came to be. I hope the words on these pages move you someday, if not today. No, it won't all make sense to you to-

day, but it'll make sense when it needs to. Whoever you are, hopefully, this is your sign.
   - Khalil Ishmael

You are exactly where you need to be.

Nobody knows
what they're doing.

When I started this book this was actually the original title I had in mind. I had absolutely no idea what it would become, but I kept writing and adding until it became something I was happy with. Nobody knows what they're doing or who they'll be. Not me. Not your parents. Not even your favorite celebrities. We're all winging this shit. Hell, most of us don't even know what we're gonna have for dinner tonight. But I'm here to tell you that this is completely okay.

This book was supposed to be a lot of things. A self-help book, a photo book, an interactive journal, a collection of things I've always wanted to tweet, etc. But as humans, we are constantly changing. Most ideas and words don't stick because we're never the same person we were when they were first created.

I don't know where I'll be tomorrow, nor do I know how I'll feel tomorrow, I don't even know *who* I'll be tomorrow, and that's okay. Most of us are still figuring things out, and even when we think we have it all figured out, life will remind us that we don't. Embrace the uncertainty of this thing called life, cause it's not going anywhere.

"You don't need validation from others to know you are worthy." - Kabriya

It's okay to not know everything.

It's cool. We've all been there. But the truth is— you don't know everything. Nobody knows everything. In fact, we hardly ever know much of anything. Sometimes we give ourselves way too much credit. We think we're stronger and smarter than we actually are (usually a lot more than we actually are), but that's never the case.

It's important that you don't know everything, actually. Acknowledging that you don't know much makes you a lot more human. As humans, we are social creatures by nature that learn and feed on the energy of each other. So when you convince yourself that you know more than others, you are subconsciously halting your path to growth and connection.

So next time, even when you think you know something, just listen. You never know what you can learn by accepting and acknowledging your lack of knowing.

"be more interested in understanding others than being understood."

Fall in love with yourself.

I asked the question "what do you do when you feel ugly?" on an Instagram poll a long time ago and received all kinds of answers. Some people cry, others gas themselves up with compliments. Some work out to numb the feeling while others put on a killer face of makeup. Some dress themselves up to remind themselves who they are. There are plenty of ways to handle this.

To put it plainly, we all experience this feeling. We've all felt ugly at some point in time, but what's important is how we react to this feeling. It's up to us to dress ourselves up and remind ourselves who we are. It's up to us to work out when we don't like what we see in the mirror. It's up to you to love yourself. No one can give you the confidence that you need like you can when you feel down. So the question isn't what do you do when you feel ugly, but:

What are you doing to fall in love with yourself?

Sometimes our feelings don't pass until we allow them to. Believe it or not, even the negative emotions can be pushed through simply by acting against them. The next time you feel ugly, weak, or just down bad, act on it. Feeling sorry for yourself won't improve your quality of life and you cannot hate yourself into a version that you love

"Life isn't easy but it's worth living." - Kiauna Rome

Pain is a natural occurrence.

Recognizing that you've hurt people is just as important as recognizing that you've been hurt. Acknowledging this makes you human. Some people live their entire lives without ever holding themselves accountable. Not every form of hurt is intentional, but we all still hurt people. We'll all hurt someone, just as we'll all be hurt by someone. This is an undeniable fact. But this doesn't excuse us from accountability.

So what about you? If you can think of any instance this is your chance to check in with them. Text, call, DM, whatever. Sure, this shows that you've grown and that you've changed, but this isn't to mend a broken friendship or to get back with your ex. This is for all parties involved – it's an opportunity to release something.

You never know how long someone will hold onto something. Words and actions will always last much longer than the physical pains that we endure. By reaching out you're releasing the person (or people) that you've hurt from the pain that they've held onto. At the same time you're releasing yourself from the weight of past actions, so think deep on it. Did a past situation have to end the way it did? Did the energy of yesterday have to be carried into today? Release yourself and others from the hurt of yesterday. We all deserve that.

Your words hold weight.

The power of the tongue is real. If someone tells you something long enough you'll start to believe it. The same can be said for what you tell yourself. If you call yourself dumb or unworthy long enough, your mind will start to believe it. You see, the thing is, your words are binding contracts with your perceived reality whether they come from a place of intent or not. So yeah, this means no more self-deprecating jokes or statements. The moment you say something you release the energy of your words into your reality, even if you don't really mean it.

So be mindful of what you say to yourself as well as others. Your words are the same as ink from a pen. When you speak it is immediately written and cannot be erased. You can't take back what you say, ever. So be wise with your words.

By this same logic, you are able to bring forth any reality you see fit. You can speak anything into your life and the lives of others, so why not speak your words in the right direction?

"It could all be over in a second." - Rajah

What do you value?

There's no wrong answer here. You could say friendship, food, music, the internet, possessions, and so on. Whatever it is should truly mean something to you. Now, take that away. How detrimental would a lack of these things be to you? Two weeks without contact from close friends? A month without music? Whatever you said, take it away. Time without the things that mean the most to you will teach you something about yourself. The things that you believed meant the world to you could mean nothing to you after some time away, but by that same logic, they could mean even more than what you believed as well.

So what do your values mean to you? It's a tough question, yes, but it's also a necessary one. You don't have to have an answer immediately, because there is a way to answer this, but it's not easy. The fact that you're reading this now is more than enough proof that you're capable.

I challenge you to a fast. It can be something of your choice, but I recommend something that you value. It can be a day, a week, or even a month. Whatever feels right for you is just fine.

A while back I took a two-week fast from music, and it was one of the most challenging things I've ever done. I loved music so much that it was practically a part of my identity. Unfortunately, I still didn't value it. Music had always been a part of my conscious life, so I never knew what life would be like without it.

Initially, I struggled. I was frustrated dealing with my thoughts and the silence around me was almost deafening. I started calling friends more and even held conversations with strangers. I honestly thought I was going crazy until I realized that this was happening because I used music to drown out the world around me. Music was my escape, but no one can stay on vacation forever. At the moment of realization, I chose to embrace the silence and all my thoughts that came with it. Everything became clear and I enjoyed the real world a bit more.

I started the fast with 10,000 songs. Today, I only have about 3,000 and it constantly changes. At the end of my fast, my taste in music changed so much that most of what I heard I didn't like anymore. So I started deleting what I didn't like or what didn't resonate with me anymore. I realized that I simply had attachments to some of these songs. Maybe they were connected to heartbreak or a good day in 2012, but that did nothing for the Khalil of 2021. So I let them go. Things like old songs come back around when you need to hear them anyway.

You can't know what you value until you've gone without it. No ifs, and, or buts. Take that break from something you think you value today. Pay attention to what you think about. Pay attention to how you occupy your time without the things you value.

So I say all of this to say: **Let that shit go.**

Don't discourage yourself and prevent growth because you're afraid to embrace change, or because you don't want to let go of what means so much to you. You just have to do it. What is for you will be for you, and who you will be is who you will be, so just accept the reality. Accept change.

Figure out what you want to let go of and give it some time. There is nothing on this planet that you are incapable of. You just have to do it. It may not be easy, but nothing truly good for you will come easily.

I'd wish you luck, but you won't need it. Nothing is off the table and nothing is impossible for you.

June 9, 2021 at 2:54 PM

Addressing unhealthy attachments

Attachment is not just limited to relationships. This also includes your lifestyle choices and vices as well.
People will **tell you** that they want better for themselves and when you give them routes to do so, they will immediately bring up how hard it is to let go of whatever is keeping them from the betterment that they seek.

When you think of doing better for yourself and how hard it'll be to let go of something in the process, that is an attachment. Now, it is more than likely an unhealthy one because you hesitated at the thought of losing it. But is it impossible to go without it?

Ask yourself why you're so attached to the thing that you stumbled over? Is it actually a necessity? How long has it been in your life?

Does it belong in your life or are you attached to it?

"Just shut up and vibe." - Cait

We're all learning.

We're all human. We're all living, learning, and making mistakes. We're all doing the best that we can. Even the people who've hurt you are learning. Maybe not as fast as you'd like them to, but they're learning nonetheless. They go through the motions of life just as you do. Yeah, they might have hurt you in the worst possible way, but if they actually knew better, they'd do better. Whatever they did to you never would've happened otherwise. The same way you never would've hurt the people you've hurt. Hurt people, hurt people. And yeah, it's corny, but as I said earlier: we've all hurt people. All that matters is that you recognize your mistakes as learning experiences.

Each mistake is simply a mistake until you make it an opportunity to become a better version of yourself. To grow, one must learn from their mistakes. Internalization is important for personal growth, but this is learned, not taught. Take this as a sign to start internalizing the turnout of situations and interactions. When you learn from your wrongdoings you understand the wrongdoings of others a little more.

So does that mean forgive your ex for treating you like shit? Kind of. Should you excuse yourself from any past wrongdoings and act like they never happened? Not really, because that's not how accountability works. Does that mean letting go of the pain of the past so that you can move forward? Definitely.

Everybody is trying even when it doesn't seem like it. So don't take shit personally. Because we're all doing our best, even when it doesn't seem like it.

"Always go with your first mind. That gut instinct when facing difficult decisions is usually the best decision you'll make." – Caleb

It is what it is.

If it's meant for you, it will be for you. If not, it will not last nor will you ever have it. Accept this. This goes for relationships, job opportunities, and anything in life that you may have a strong wanting for. While the sentiment of being upset about not getting something you really want is understandable, there will never be a time in your life where you can control anything in your life other than yourself. It is what it is.

You cannot make someone love you. You cannot force someone to hire you. You cannot control anything other than the actions you take. You have to give in to this, or you will forever be let down and torn apart by the things that were never for you in the first place. Life will always play out the way it wants. This doesn't mean you can't make your own decisions. It just means that you have to be ready to accept the things that you cannot change. The reality we want is hardly ever the reality that is.

Accept what is meant for you and reject all that is not. This too is a form of self-love.

"There's not a weapon in this world that can be formed against you that you don't have the ability to defeat."
— Duryan Flie

"There are no do-overs." – Iris Griffith

Live for you, take chances, and never stop creating
– Brennan Sanders

Did you take a breath today?

Consider this: the internet didn't become available to everyone until 1993 (and to most it still wasn't accessible), and before that, we only received info on the world from the news (newspaper/tv/radio) and word of mouth. Now we have the news in our hands every day. We have access to the entire world in the palm of our hands. We take in so much every day. Especially with the grip that social media and the internet have on us. There's funny stuff on Twitter and Instagram, sure, but it's still a lot. There's discourse, tragedy and more that we now see everyday.

Now let's factor in your daily life. You work, try to maintain a social life, take care of yourself, handle things as they arise, and survive. Life really is a lot. So give yourself a break. Put your phone down. Turn off your music. Stop whatever you're doing and just breathe. Even if it's for a second, just breathe and relax. You haven't taken any time for yourself today. Give your mind and heart a second to catch up.

You need to breathe. You deserve the peace of mind. Even if it's for a second, it could change your entire day.

"Enjoy life." - Joe

Life doesn't stop moving. No matter how good or bad it gets. Keep moving forward. "
– Shunydra

Dispel your doubt.

Who told you that you weren't capable? That you didn't belong where you are today? That you can't do anything that you set your mind to? Who told you that you're small and powerless? Do you believe them?

There will be moments when you feel small. Moments where you may feel like you aren't enough or don't do enough. Maybe there are moments where you feel like you don't have what it takes to walk down the path you're on. But the reality is: you're walking down the path right now. You are living through it at this very moment. You have it in you and it's always been in you.

Take a second and think about all the wins in your life. Think about the moments when you didn't think you'd make it through and still stood tall at the end of it all. Think about the hell that you endured to get to where you are today. Even if that means just surviving, you are here. That's a win. No matter how big or small, a win is a win.

You are here today. You didn't end up where you are on accident. You are capable of accomplishing anything. You are powerful and nothing is off the table. Dispel the doubt that lies within you and in turn, you will dispel the doubt that lies within others.

Do you ever get tired of fighting
Against those who make you question yourself?
They might try to take & take & take from you,
But some of your weapons they simply never can:
The undying art you put into our world,
& the beauty you've yet to uncover.
Your heart for others,
Some of who you might not even know yet.
& your love for yourself,
Some of which you might not even know yet.
– Nevay

Nothing is easy. Nothing is gonna fall in your lap. Enjoy the process. —Stoney Jackson

You are not an impostor. You didn't end up where you are on accident. You belong in every space you occupy.

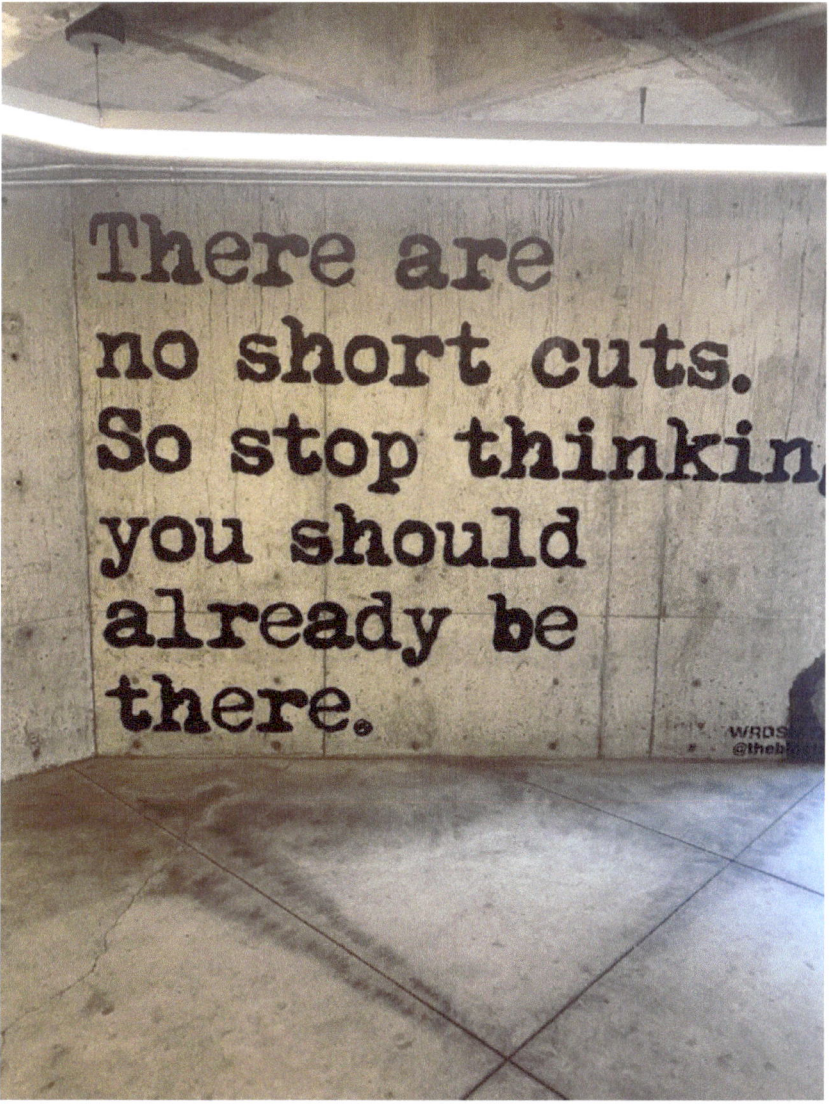

Don't let society define what success looks like.
—Tyren

You will fail.

You will fail. You will fail so fucking hard sometimes that you'll want to stop whatever it is you're pursuing. Even the most prolific athletes and revered artists have failed. But that doesn't make them any less amazing. The bottom line is: You will be dogshit terrible at something before you are ever any good at it.

I've been doing photography for almost ten years now. And even after all this time has passed, my least favorite part of the photography process is getting home, opening Lightroom, and seeing all of my mistakes from a freshly finished shoot. It is the most humbling thing you have to deal with as a photographer. Screw Instagram likes and people not tagging you in photos. There's nothing like having your mistakes laid out in front of you. But what's crucial in this very vulnerable moment is that you internalize what's going wrong in the process. This is something that you have to do not only as a photographer, but any walk of life. You have to embrace these failures. So the shitty lighting and editing mistakes I made in 2015 won't reappear in 2021. But if I never made these mistakes and recognized them, how would I have grown as a photographer?

There is no such thing as talent. Only skill. This means that the magnitude of "perfection" that you seek in whatever it is that you do will not come without some practice, execution, and falling flat on your fucking face. So don't be afraid to fail. Embrace the failure and do your best to internalize it. Ask yourself what you can do better after every attempt at growth. I say growth because that's what it actually is. The effort that you put forward is contributing to you growing into whatever it is that you want to be.

Life is too short to be afraid. Grab life by the horns and take chances. Live to the fullest!
– Nakia Bolden

"Appreciate the journey and don't cheat the process."
—Adrianna

It's okay to change your mind.

I can't tell you how many times I've felt like an idiot for telling people my life plans only for them to change at the drop of a dime. But it took me a long time to realize that this is okay. Life moves fast— like unbelievably fast. And the entire time that life is doing its thing, you're changing. You're experiencing new things, meeting new people, seeing new sights, and so much more. These very things reshape you as a person every day. You aren't even the same person you were when you started reading this book.

So never feel bad when something doesn't feel right for the current you. It's impossible to know what will happen tomorrow or even a week from now. We make choices as best as we can with what we are given today alongside what we think tomorrow will bring. But that never means anything has to be set in stone.

People may see you as indecisive, but that's okay. No one knows what's best for you like you do. So when you find yourself feeling like a failure or an indecisive embarrassment, remember that of course, nobody knows what they're doing. But also, the only thing that's certain is that nothing is certain.

Find what makes you happy and do it. – Jasmine

There's no such thing as perfection or perfect timing, only success. – Sully

Gentle reminder:
Be as kind to yourself as you are to others.

The world will still
be here tomorrow.

I promise you, the world isn't going anywhere. Take your time when you wake up in the morning. Stretch. Read a little bit. Take a breath and ground yourself. Take your time when you sip your coffee. Watch the sunrise if you need to. Just make time for you to start your day. You're always in control of how you handle the day. Everything else? Not so much.

Ground yourself. You are in control of your reality. Not your job or the plans you have for the day. The goal is to fall in love with yourself, the circumstances of the day, and your reality before you ever leave home. When you rush yourself out the door, you make room for the fragility of reality; allowing your peace to be shattered from the slightest disturbance. This means you're more likely to get road rage or be emotionally swayed by something minor in nature. Stability is important for a good mental foundation, and you can't get that without proper preparation. So just relax, the world isn't going anywhere.

Never take for granted the limited time you have on this earth, or the important people you have in your life. Make the most of every moment, live in the now, and prepare for the future because nothing stays the same for too long. People, places, and things you've grown accustomed to won't always be around so cherish them while they're here and take advantage of the opportunities available to you because time waits for no one.

We are here today and gone tomorrow so create a life you won't regret.
– Kris

Live.

Alright, let's get a hypothetical going: You're retiring at 65 years old, and you've lived pretty much all your life in accordance with the social norms we're bound to. You lived all 65 years in fear of disappointing your friends, family, and peers, so you avoided doing the things you were genuinely interested in or were afraid to try. Now you're 65 with plenty of health problems and commitments and it's harder than ever to do the things you wanted to do in your younger years because of this. Your life is filled with regret from all the opportunities you missed out on and the experiences you didn't have, due to fear. You now ask yourself every day: "Was it worth it?"

That's a reality for a lot of people. You've always had the power to decide what you do with your life. Your life is yours, so go ahead and live the way you want to. Not how your parents or peers think you should, but how *you* think you should. Fill your life with the things that make you happy. Do the things that you dream of doing. Visit the places you see on Instagram. Go live. Live like you're going to die. Live like there is no meaning to our existence because there will come a day (sooner than you think) where you won't be able to anymore.

Live life to the fullest.
– Damian

You'll figure it out along the way.

The truth about happiness is that it's not constant. It's not a state that you stay in all your life. You're still experiencing life. The things that make you happy will change just as you do. You might outgrow a few things, and that's okay. Just keep living. None of this is set in stone, remember? You might not even know what makes you happy right now, but that's okay. You'll figure it out along the way. The worst thing you can do is wait for happiness to find you.

It's worth remembering that most of us spend *at least* the first quarter of our lives appeasing others. So if you're just now starting your search for happiness, be patient. You might not even know who you really are just yet. Life is a lot of things, but above all else, it is the ultimate learning experience. You're learning who you are, as well as who you aren't. Along the way, you'll try new things and you might not like them, but the process of elimination is still a process nonetheless.

You might think you know who you are today, but you never know who you'll be tomorrow. Go skydiving, dye your hair, start traveling, whatever you think will bring you happiness and comfort in this bleak world, go do it. Chase what you feel and embrace the uncertainty.

Leave no stone unturned. Life is just about that: living.

Be a better person than yesterday. – Kamarri

Money isn't the key to happiness, not by a long shot.
– Allen P. Griffith

It's okay to put yourself first.

Most have gone their entire lives putting the wellbeing (and opinions) of others above their own. Putting the perspective of others above your own means relinquishing the control you have over your reality. In order to preserve the quality of life that you desire you must always put yourself first and do what's best for you.

Sounds simple enough. Most times it won't be easy to make a big decision, but if you keep this in mind, you'll never fumble. Oftentimes what's best for you might be the hardest thing to do, but it will never be impossible. Forget about the risks and sacrifices. The only thing that matters here is what leaves you in the best position. If you follow this logic, you'll never go wrong.

But don't just apply this to life-changing decisions. Always do what's best for you. That's what self-care actually is. Prioritizing yourself and always putting yourself in a winning position. If quitting the job that you hate is what you feel is best for you, do it. If you don't have the energy for a relationship (platonic or not), then do what's best for you and create space. You cannot live for others, and others cannot live for you. So you must make yourself your #1 priority. Otherwise, you'll always come second to everyone and everything else. No matter what it is you want, you have to put yourself first and do what's best for you. The you of tomorrow will thank you.

A year from now you'll wish you started today.
   - Katie Swain

Take in every moment and always take pictures.
– J'La

You are what you eat.

What you eat is important, yeah, but you feed yourself in other ways. From the shows you watch and the music you listen to, to the people you talk to every day and the people you follow on social media.

You know how most people get upset over the Instagram algorithm because it doesn't arrange the timeline in chronological order? That's a great example of your diet. It's a direct reflection of who and what you watch the most on the app. This is who (or what) you look at and interact with the most. You ever think about why some people call their timelines "the feed?" This is why. It's up to you to be more selective with your time and energy. You are what you eat, so if all you see on the timeline is negativity, eventually you will become negative in nature as well. Apply this to food, relationships, how you spend your time, and more.

You are your most important asset, so you have to take care of yourself. To lead a positive life you should fill it with positive things. The more the better. Remember: If it's not helping you, it could be hurting you.

You deserve the best in every sense.

There's enough for everyone, and you're always enough for yourself. Everything else? That's just life. —Tsukiyomi

"Keep in touch with yourself.
The kettle boils long before it releases the steam."
– Courtney

See the good in every situation.

Yes, at first glance optimism seems dumb and unrealistic. but why choose to be sad or bothered when you have a more productive option? You see a mistake as a failure when it should be a moment for learning. You see a lack of something in your life as a reflection of character, instead of something you can work to attain. Stop looking at the glass as half-empty. This does everything for you and it does absolutely nothing for you.

So yeah, at first glance life is "hard", but in reality, that's just life. There will always be challenges and stressors, but don't let this be the reason that you forget all the good that comes from life. It's important to remain positive because dampening your outlook on life only makes things harder than they have to be.

Take this as a sign to stop seeing failed relationships as failures when they're lessons to be learned. Stop seeing setbacks as your life falling apart, when they're just the motions of life. It's tough to adapt to things, but it's not impossible. There is light at the end of the tunnel so long as you want it to be there.

Breathe positivity into your life, because no one else can do that for you. No one can make things better for you, nor can they make things happen for you. *You* have to be the change that you seek. This is your reality, remember?

If you can manage your money
you'll have an easier life.
– Jalen

"Live how you want. Not the way others dictate."
– Khali

Change is the only constant.

It's okay to change, I promise. The only thing that is constant in this world is that nothing is constant. Think about it like this: we are living in history. Something new happens every day. There are new inventions, words, and developments every day. There are changes in our shared reality every day. Nothing stays the same, so why should you?

For some reason, we romanticize what is way too often. We want things to always stay the same. We want to keep our friends close and our lives consistent, but that's not the world we're living in. Life is one big ball that never stops rolling, so neither should you. Change is going to happen whether you want it to or not, and the best thing you can do is just accept that. Be prepared to change with the world, or inevitably be left behind.

You are not supposed to be the same person forever. That's how growth works. We'll grow apart from our friends and family, but we'll grow into new ones. We'll outgrow hobbies, habits, and interests. We must embrace change because it's one of the only constants we have in this world. You must embrace who you'll be tomorrow and what the world will offer you because that is a reality that we cannot change. To reject change is to reject growth, and to reject growth is to reject who you are meant to be.

Life is irreplaceable.
Because of that, I believe in nurturing my energy- reflect, stay present, & daydream.
In reality, the importance of expressing emotions is substantial- mental health, hobbies, & immediate relationships. so in the end do what feels right & you will live a good life.
- Sydney

You can't fix the past, but you can live right now for a better future. –Ty

Comfort can breed complacency.
Give yourself the opportunity to be uncomfortable
and navigate outside of your own box.
– Koopa

Blow your money regularly and recklessly, because you never know when it's gon' be over.
And have some savings for your kids cause hopefully they live longer than you do.
– Isaiah Rashad

Your will is your own.

When I first started the book I was doing my best to make something that would spark change in others. To say the least there was a lot of ego and forcefulness behind the words. As I read them over and over again I realized what was wrong. I realized that I am powerless. I thought I had more influence and pull than I actually do. I thought I had the power to change the world, but the truth is: No one can change anyone. Your will belongs to you, and you alone. You can't force it onto others.

It's not your job (or your place) to try and change people. No matter what you do, learn, or know, you only have control over your reality. Even this book and all the things you learn from it are not things to force onto others. When people want to change, they'll change. They're just waiting for their next sign. The same as you and me. So when you share this book with a friend, don't tell them there's a specific page for them. Let them find it on their own. It's only a sign if when you see it as one.

About the Author

You're pretty much at the end of the book. Kudos to you for seeing it through. There are only a few more pages before you actually finish, but I wanted to tell you a bit about myself before you finish up. Nobody told me that this would be the hardest part of writing a book. It took me a while to figure it out, but after countless attempts... here we go.

Khalil Griffith was born and raised in Little Rock, Arkansas. By the time he could remember anything, his parents weren't together, so he bounced between both homes for a large portion of his upbringing. Because of this, Khalil experienced both poverty and privilege in his early years, but he never went un-loved. At best, he was an average student. He was undoubtedly intelligent and creative, but he didn't have any interest in academics. He made decent grades so long when he applied himself, but he had a hard time due to a lack of interest. During his first year of high school, he discovered the blogging app, Tumblr, and developed a genuine interest in photography from there. He started taking photos on an iPod touch his parents got him for his birthday in an attempt to replicate the images he saw on the internet. He was definitely an amateur, but this was the first creative spark he'd experienced. With the assistance of image-based platforms like VSCO and Instagram, his eye for photography grew stronger over the years.

The time flew by and before he knew it, he was graduating from Little Rock Central High School. He had no idea what he wanted to do for a career, but he knew he had to pick something. He had thoughts of being a psychologist, going to the military, and so on before he landed on the idea of being a marine biologist. He knew it was a bit far-fetched but stuck with it since it would make everyone around him happy with him. Khalil was lucky enough to receive financial aid that would cover the cost of his college career at the University of Arkansas at Little Rock. Most of his scholarships came from his decision to major in biology. This was the beginning of the end.

To be frank, he wasn't doing well in college. He was hardly ever making it to class, he was depressed, and his grades weren't anything to brag about. He knew something wasn't right but he couldn't put his finger on it. No matter how many alarms he set, he couldn't bring himself to make it to class on time. No matter how hard he studied, it seemed that it wasn't good enough. It didn't all make sense for him until he dropped a science course. As much as he liked science, he didn't see himself being in this field for the rest of his life. He realized that this wasn't even remotely close to how he envisioned his life. At this point, he wanted to do something that he had a genuine interest in and decided photography was the route he'd take. He had no idea how he'd explain this sudden decision to anyone, especially his parents, but it didn't matter. He was doing what he thought was best for him. In turn, he lost every scholarship he had and from that point forward he had to pay for school out of pocket. But all this disappointment meant nothing if he was following his heart.

As it turns out, he sucked at school no matter what topic it was. Eventually, he couldn't afford to stay in school anymore without financial assistance so he dropped out. During this time away from school, he worked, dove into photography and other forms of art, and actually started experiencing life outside of academia. He had no idea what life was like outside of school so he took it all in. After some time passed, he decided that he'd come up with a plan, go back to school, and get a good job somewhere. The dream, right? Well, school sucked just as much as before, but this time was different. He made better grades, never missed classes, and felt like things were actually working out how they should've been all along. The only problem was... it didn't feel like him.

Khalil spent the past 22 years of his life appeasing others. Going to college, working a job that he hated, giving up all of his time for someone else... all of this just to fit in. It didn't sit right with him. This was the turning point. This was when he decided that he'd carve his own path into the world and live life the way he wanted to. Not the way his parents or society thought he should. This was the moment that Khalil Griffith died.

Khalil's Sign

It's been about three years since then, and a lot's happened. I've traveled across the country, met a countless number of people from around the world, crossed things off my bucket list, wrote a book, and more. Today, you can find me on just about any social media platform under the name of Khalil Ishmael creating something or passionately sharing my heartfelt opinion. I could tell you all the random things about me like what I like to do in my free time, where I want to be, or what my favorite food is, but I don't think it's necessary. By the time you read this, I might not even be the same person. I believe in seeing things for myself and forming my own opinions and shaping my reality based on the things I experience, so I encourage you to do the same.

Most people know me as a photographer, but honestly, I'm just a guy that takes pictures. I'm technically an author now, but I'm not a writer, I'm just a guy that wrote a book. I don't like the idea of these titles because they make things sound much further off than they are. No, you don't have 10 years of photography experience under your belt, but you could start taking photos today and be featured in a magazine tomorrow. Hell, I had zero writing experience before creating this book and it took me months to get to this page, but I did it. So I guess now is as good of a time as any to give you my sign.

Don't fret about what others think as long as you're following your heart. You can do anything. You are the god of your reality and you are in complete control of where and how far you go. No matter what is in your heart, so long as you have the will and courage to do it you will come out on top.

– Khalil Ishmael (2:22pm)

An Expression of Gratitude

Thank you. Thank you for being you. Thank you for never getting anything done. Thank you for the sense of direction you never had. Thank you for counting yourself out. Thank you for always falling short. Thank you for not knowing what the fuck you're doing.

Until next time, friend.

Hopefully, this was your sign.

www.ingramcontent.com/pod-product-compliance
Lightning Source LLC
Chambersburg PA
CBHW042236090526
44589CB00006B/74